11/13/22

To ashley,

Turn your sorrow

treasured gold ~ Au

Love,

Deb

Merciful, I Am

The Story of How Forgiving Others
Taught Me How to Forgive Myself

DEBORAH A. BOULEY

BALBOA.
PRESS
A DIVISION OF HAY HOUSE

Balboa Press books may be ordered through booksellers or by contacting:

Balboa Press
A Division of Hay House
1663 Liberty Drive
Bloomington, IN 47403
www.balboapress.com
1 (877) 407-4847

Because of the dynamic nature of the Internet, any web addresses or links contained in this book may have changed since publication and may no longer be valid. The views expressed in this work are solely those of the author and do not necessarily reflect the views of the publisher, and the publisher hereby disclaims any responsibility for them.

The author of this book does not dispense medical advice or prescribe the use of any technique as a form of treatment for physical, emotional, or medical problems without the advice of a physician, either directly or indirectly. The intent of the author is only to offer information of a general nature to help you in your quest for emotional and spiritual well-being. In the event you use any of the information in this book for yourself, which is your constitutional right, the author and the publisher assume no responsibility for your actions.

Any people depicted in stock imagery provided by Getty Images are models, and such images are being used for illustrative purposes only. Certain stock imagery © Getty Images.

Print information available on the last page.

ISBN: 978-1-9822-0548-5 (sc)
ISBN: 978-1-9822-0547-8 (hc)
ISBN: 978-1-9822-0549-2 (e)

Library of Congress Control Number: 2018906641

Balboa Press rev. date: 06/25/2018

And You Shall Be Called
Salina
(Sa-Lee-Nah)
Translation: Merciful

Merciful (Opposite of Cruel)
Forgiving, Compassionate, Humane, Lenient,
Kind, Softhearted, Tenderhearted, Gracious,
Benevolent, Relieving a Person's Pain

Especially when you are in a position to
punish them or treat them harshly

DEDICATION

This book is dedicated to the little girl inside me
who was not heard for a long, long time.

It is also dedicated to Patty Lane, who first
heard her whispers and listened carefully.

CONTENTS

Contents

INTRODUCTION

WHEN I WATCH ANIMALS parenting their offspring, I am always struck by the thought that they instinctively know how to do it. They don't read How-To books and articles. They don't have the newest gadgets to assist them. They don't have nannies or coaches. They just do it naturally. And yet some humans, perhaps many humans, do not know how to do it easily, if at all.

How do we learn how to parent well? Is it by watching good role models? What happens if there are no positive role models, except the ones on TV, who only show snippets of skill? As a child growing up in the late fifties and early sixties, I looked to June Cleaver for guidance on how a good mother behaves. Later on I watched Mrs. Cunningham on "Happy Days" to discern more clues. Neither woman fits in today's world; or do they?

Can we learn from resource materials? Maybe, but what if something happens that is not categorized in the books? How many people intentionally research parenting and apply what they read to their real lives? I suspect many people have the best of intentions, but their familial history and internal dialogue limits what they are able to actually do.

The shame I consistently felt as a kid flowed effortlessly through me, and became engrained in who I was and what I was worth. It was a normal and comfortable feeling for me. I felt shame for the behaviors and actions of my parents. I felt shame for what they did to other people. I felt shame that I was born into this unit. I always knew that the way I lived was not how other kids in my school lived. The little girl inside of me was never safe, always on guard to live a defensive life, until very recently. I would not at all be surprised if my classmates from elementary, middle and high school are shocked by my secrets. I learned early on that the way to survive was to pretend that bad things did not happen, and to try to blend in with the crowd, so as not to stick out. Secrets are what kept the masquerade going.

After decades of my own research I now believe that my parents did the best that they could with what they knew or believed to be true at the time. I understand how cycles of abuse happen, how generational flaws are passed down and repeated. I now believe that my parents were trapped into repeating what was modeled for them. I never saw my mother take any accountability for anything she did. It was as if she was always right – no guilt and no remorse - ever. I think my Dad knew more. I believe he was tormented by his own behavior, acknowledged it, but was unable to stop it. I believe his was the harder life because he saw glimpses of right behavior in himself that would then evaporate without warning, and later leave him with guilt pulsing in his veins.

Over the last seventeen years or so I finally came to believe that I could be more than I was, and so I set my own path based on what I felt God wanted for me. Fear of many things, including disloyalty to the family unit, by acknowledging and telling secrets, made this process difficult, and at times agonizing. However, my faith that I can do all things through Christ who strengthens me (Phillipians 4:13, ESV), allowed me to accept that I am worthy and deserving of a wonderful life. And so I set my soul free.

I loved both my parents. I was always hopeful that something could change someday. I would often think that maybe one day I could be safe and exhale. No matter how awful an incident would be I would think first that they didn't mean it, or didn't mean for it to happen, and the next thought was that I couldn't tell anyone because my parents would be hurt by it. I didn't want them punished, because I felt that they couldn't help doing it. I just wanted them to stop. Even when I said that I was done, fed up, wouldn't entertain hope and would armor myself up further, somewhere deep down inside I would think that it wouldn't happen again. But, it always did.

God, Spirit, Higher Power, always brought me comfort,

even when I was a little, little girl. No one taught me about a Higher Power, but I knew that I had the strength and determination deep inside of me to endure for the purpose of bringing a greater good to the world. I just knew at some inner level that God was giving me testimonies so that I could be a comfort and teacher to others.

I was born in August 1957 without a first name. My mother told me that on her second day in the hospital, she got a roommate who gave birth to a daughter she named Deborah. I was given her name because she couldn't think of a name for me. No mention was ever made of my father's involvement in naming me, however, years later when I learned about how he discovered his real name, it did not surprise me that he did not participate in my naming. When I was first told this story as a child I did not feel forgotten, or unprepared for, or unwanted exactly. It seemed to be a befitting story for a child who never felt that she belonged. I considered myself to be a child of God. It was a feeling that He was always with me and that no matter how bad things got He would not abandon me. Looking back on this now I am amazed how I knew this or believed this. I was sent to CCD, as it was called (Catholic Religious Education), so that I could make my Communion and Confirmation, but I never learned about a relationship with Jesus. Now I know that Deborah was a prophet and the only female judge mentioned in the Bible. She also wrote a victory song, which is part of the Book of Judges. I am honored to share her name and more honored to proclaim myself a child of God.

Times were different back then. A few years ago, I started to become aware of the challenges of being born in the late fifties and living now. Behaviors that were acceptable then are not now. I realized that I live in two different worlds. There was the world I was raised in, the values that I was either born into or brought into, and the world of now which showed me that my thinking was flawed.

Back then children were commonly slapped and physically punished. I was trained to be silent. I was raised with discipline and fear, and taught to not question why. Men were the heads of households and established rules for the women and children to abide by. Sometimes the women obeyed, and sometimes they became subversive. They did what they wanted to or dared to "on the sneak". Black eyes were hidden behind sunglasses. What happened behind closed doors, stayed behind closed doors. People minded their own business even if they knew someone was getting abused or terrorized.

There were no "openly gay people" as they remained closeted. There were no visible unwed mothers in high school, as they were shuttled away to secretly have their babies and then give them up for adoption. There were no visible interracial couples.

Women were expected to be wives and mothers. They

prepared for this life plan much more than they ever prepared for a career. In the 1970s, women learned that they could have careers, but only if they held the roles of wife and mother as well. Women of my time endured. Many times I would arise very early and prepare the house, ready the children, etc. and drive an hour to work where I would work diligently and hard for several hours. I don't remember taking lunch breaks, but do remember driving the hour back home exhausted. Once home I would cook and clean and do laundry and bathe the kids and the many other tasks. I had no breathe because I gave it all away.

The Civil Rights Movement and the Women's Movement did much to improve the lives of women, but from my perspective, it was the advent of technology that really changed the world. Technology allowed me to see how other people actually lived, pretended to live, or wished that they lived. It is through technology that I learned there are other grown children like me who have lived similar lives. The advent of technology allowed me to explore without judgment. It provided me a connection I never had before.

I have been a high school teacher in an inner city school for a while now. I have watched the changes in expectations evolve. Each day I watch young people interact with their phones far more than they ever interact with humans directly. Their perception of hardship is very different than mine.

Kids today are very forthcoming. I realized long ago that

I had been trained to keep secrets. The secrets killed me. I've known for a long time that I needed to tell my stories, as I experienced them, in order to take away their power. It's not the stories so much that harmed me, but the feelings that I have attached to the stories. I am of the belief that we enter the world with feelings we draw from our mothers. We share the same bodies for nine months, so why not the same anguish or joy. Some of us are born with burdens we didn't ask for nor deserve.

I have worked very hard, over four decades, to free myself from my old tapes. My old tapes were the stories I told myself about how I was not good enough, not worthy enough, not important enough to have feelings or desires. They were born from the lessons I learned about what it means to be the child of parents who were unable to parent. There were many events that influenced who I became and how I behaved, but I clearly heard God tell me to talk first about the particular seven I write about in this book.

The chapters may not bring you comfort as you read them, but I hope when you are finished reading you can feel the resiliency and strength that can exist in horrible circumstances. The last chapter is intended to bring all who are suffering proof that your past does not define you.

Thank you for listening to the stories of a girl who once had no voice, and had no one who would have believed her if she had spoken. It took me an extremely long time to find my voice and understand that I was not betraying my family by breaking patterns of behavior. Instead I was creating new, helpful next best steps for myself in a glorious life that I deserve.

Today I have three names. My birth name is "Deborah," but I was given the name of "Truth" this summer at a tipping point workshop. This workshop enabled me to see that I had enough strength and courage to tip the scales and tell the truth. Truth is what I have sought my whole life. I left this event with the official new name of "Salina." Salina represents the forgiveness and mercy I have given to others, and myself, and it is this mercy that has allowed my rebirth to happen.

CHAPTER 1

Forty Years of Therapy

FORTY YEARS OF THERAPY. Forty years of sometimes being in a state of confusion and isolation, not knowing how to just be, and sometimes, in fleeting moments, clearly seeing the answers I sought and then losing them, sort of like puffs of smoke that vanished. It is like being in a perpetual fog, knowing that I am a little lost, but very hopeful that the fog will lift one day soon and I will be able to see what is in front of me, what is behind me, and appreciate right where I am.

As I approached the age of 60 last August, some things were crystal clear to me. I knew that I was tired of being frustrated and was ready to fit the pieces of the puzzle of my life together. No longer did it suit me to be a fragmented, disconnected set of parts, seemingly unrelated to one another. It was time to take all the ingredients I had gathered, cultivated, and nurtured over a lifetime and whip them together into the most delicious masterpiece of Deb Bouley.

I have suffered from anxiety my whole life, and am convinced now that it actually began before my birth, from conception. It is generational, passed down from one person to the next in utero. My mother resented being pregnant because it forced her to gain weight, and that was sinful. My mother suffered from beliefs that were not Christian – let's leave that here for now. There have been times when I have been a tortured, conflicted soul, consumed by the physical symptoms that I have allowed to control my life. Forty years of therapy have allowed me to understand how these symptoms are bred, which are bogus, and which require medical attention. It is hard to be me, knowing that I can cause my own misery. At the same time, it is very empowering to acknowledge that I can create my own happiness and joy. I have endured and survived the challenges in my life, and thrived from the lessons I have learned. I knew last summer that I was ready to give myself permission to release my secrets. I am strong enough and prepared enough from forty years of therapy, to challenge the defining stories I have told myself, and align them with the truth of who I am today.

I think my first memories of anxiety began at around age four or five and were feelings of danger. My parents did not get along. You will learn from my seven stories how this manifested. As I am writing this paragraph, I can actually call up the feelings of terror and imminent danger I felt then as my parents fought with one another. Back then the waves of fight-or-flight responses were a normal part of my being. I am pretty sure that a reddened face, sweaty palms, and stomach pain accompanied the first few rounds of fear, but over time these outward clues became deceptively unnoticeable to the general public. They were never acknowledged by my parents, or maybe they were not seen by them. It is not as if I only felt them when a fight was happening. These feelings were ever present because there was always the threat of something, either a fight between my parents, them with a neighbor, them with their families, and when I was alone with my mother there was always a threat of something bad happening then.

Over the course of my childhood these particular symptoms morphed into other symptoms, as the causes remained unchallenged. I threw up every morning for over a year as a young school aged child. I would go to school with a brown paper bag to vomit in as I walked alone. I stuttered terribly in public as a young child. I learned through therapy later on that my vomiting was an attempt at throwing up my feelings, and the stuttering was a representation of how I had no voice to cry out for help and rescue.

I developed a peculiar set of tics. My stomach would contract or spasm all the time. As much as I tried to hide it, it was evident to those around me. They would stare at my stomach and ask me if I was okay. Of course I said yes. Some might have labeled this as a nervous twitch. It's like when you finish sobbing uncontrollably and have that reflex to take short breaths. It happened mostly when I was with my father's family. If there were ever a group of people I might have considered telling things to as a kid, it would have been my father's sisters. I thought they were the most normal people I knew as a child, or at least the ones who might have had some power to help me. The twitches were as close as I came to being able to show my distress. Something inside of me stopped me just short of asking for help. In retrospect I now suspect that they would not have helped me. After my dad's death I learned how masterful many people are at keeping their own secrets.

It brings me great sadness to remember this little girl who had no voice and lived in terror. It was horrible to be her then. And at the same time I feel sadness, I feel such compassion for her. She has evolved into not only a survivor, but a warrior and advocate for others in need.

Over time, the tics and vomiting lessened, as did the stuttering, partly I think because I got older and stronger at controlling them. But other physical symptoms took their place. Each one presented itself as a diversion, as if to pull me away from crafting a real happy life. "Am I dying? What is wrong with me? Nothing is wrong with me—ignore it." Eventually, in my late teens, I began to experience panic attacks, the nightmare of all nightmares as far as I am concerned. They appeared seemingly out of nowhere and felt as if the end of life was near. I can only compare mine to feeling as if I were hanging by my fingernails on the wing of a plane that was flying mid-air. What made them most terrifying to me was that I could not control them, and that while having one I might be "found out". My mask would be revealed, my secrets told, and then something really bad would happen.

The fear was enough for me to surrender to therapy. I became agoraphobic for a short while. And then I grew to learn that I was in no danger, that I could manage the panic, and confront the fears and live in some facade of normalcy.

For years I held my anxiety at bay, even convinced myself that it was gone for good, like a nightmare. I did not recognize, or was unwilling to acknowledge, that I needed to reconcile the causes of my anxiety and give myself permission to be happy. Because I pretended I was okay when I wasn't, the anxiety would reappear with a vengeance during very stressful times of my life. One such time was in the spring of 2003, when I had a mini-stroke. This event changed things for me, as I anticipated having another every second of every subsequent day for years.

I had an ocular migraine, which mimicked the symptoms of my stroke, the day of my 40th high school reunion. I was in charge of remembering those students in my graduating class who had died. There was such irony in this because had I not been dead myself for so many years? I was charged with the task of eulogizing real physical death. I had all the candles and materials to set up this tribute and therefore felt trapped to attend. I remember phoning the class president and explaining I was having a panic attack and she was so gracious and thoughtful. I used my techniques from therapy to drive the hour plus down and delivered a good speech. But its intensity rattled me.

And then when my youngest daughter went away to college and I was left to figure out how to make a life for myself, I suffered a series of these.

The last two years have been particularly challenging for me as I worked very hard to acknowledge my victim stories, separate them from the feelings they bring, and forgive everyone, including myself. Two summers ago, for the first time ever, I did not work summer school. I spent a grueling month at an Airbnb on my beloved Cape Cod, reading and then writing the first threads of this book. I had anxiety attack after anxiety attack as I unpeeled my onion, layer by layer. That intense work prepared me for a year of hell at my job where I confronted many of my fears surrounding the approval of others, and living a life of other people's expectations.

I was paid attention to by people as long as I was useful to them. The minute I stopped doing what they expected of me, and tried to be true to myself, I felt abandoned. I fought very hard to create my own boundaries. These are authentic boundaries, ones that are good for Deborah.

Last spring, while my twice-a-month therapy sessions continued, it was as if I was a new student to self-discovery. It became clear that all the years of hard work, exploring, analyzing, reconciling, and understanding had cracked me open. I started to feel my armor fall away and I recognized that the war was over. I was on the precipice of something really big, but couldn't quite grasp what it might be. But I felt it as clearly as I felt the wind.

The therapy I had throughout my life was the type whereby I had to find my own answers. Patty, the very best therapist ever for me, would guide me; sort of lead me through questioning to my own answers. That takes a lot of time, patience, focus, and effort. This was, at times, a very tiring process for me, as I was never quite sure if I was on the right track or if I was going in circles. I understood that sometimes I had to row in circles before I could go forward, but last spring I knew that I was ready for something different, something to send me off in the right direction—a direction to fulfill my purpose on this planet. I was ready for what felt like a catapult, a shot out of a cannon.

Over the years, in addition to therapy and Overeaters Anonymous and Weight Watchers, I spent a lot of time reading and digesting self-help books. I never thought I was good enough. I don't think it ever even dawned on me that I might be good enough. These were not conscious thoughts. They brimmed right under the surface. I have been searching my whole life for an understanding of what normal is. I never had a measure of it. I was not exposed to normal as a kid, and struggled with any and all of my decisions in my life, questioning and re-analyzing my choices for accuracy. I followed logic because it had served me well through tight spaces.

As a kid I new that normal was foreign through my observations of the other kids. What they said, how they acted, what they wore, how they laughed clued me into being different. I was very reserved in school. I wore my coat of armor. I wanted what they had, but didn't know how to get it, and in fact couldn't even define it. In high school I had more views of normal because I started visiting other homes. I dared myself and did it. What I saw in other people's homes fascinated me, especially my friend's interactions with their families. And as a late teenager I knew I had no idea what normal was when I began having panic attacks.

Oprah Winfrey was a gift from God to me because her soulful shows tuned me into a side of life I had not "seen" before. She brought topics to the national spotlight that others pretended didn't exist. She asked great probing questions that reached to a person's soul. I had not seen "soul" or "heart" before, and had not realized that these things could be valuable. Out of all Oprah's guests, there was one in particular whom I felt totally connected to. She sang my song and I liked her style. The year was 2002, and the life coach was Iyanla Vanzant. I read her book, *In the Meantime,* and digested it for about six months. I had known for years that my marriage had died, but did not understand that in order to survive, I needed to leave it. And so I did, with great trauma and unanticipated complications. I have followed Iyanla ever since, and consider her to be my boot camp spiritual guide. An outward badass like me, needs a badass like her to get my attention.

Last spring, as I sat in anticipation of my turning point, the Holy Spirit led me to search on the Internet for summer workshops. I found that Iyanla was hosting a weeklong event during July at the Omega Institute, which was less than an hour from my house. I instinctively knew that this was where I had to be. I knew that I was ready to have someone call me out on my stories – to challenge what I called the truth for myself, and redirect me to a different, more authentic reality. I knew that Iyanla was that person for me. I called Omega and was told the workshop was booked, and I was put on a waiting list. The next day I received a phone call that I was in. To me this was further confirmation that this was fate and I was meant to learn from her face to face.

This workshop was indeed my turning point. Forty years of therapy were necessary to bring me fully to this workshop.

I needed to be open and vulnerable before I attended, so that I could receive all the love and truth that I did.

This 60th year is a pivotal year for me. I am releasing story after story and understanding why I needed to experience and hold onto each of them for so long. They each strengthened my ego – the part of me that wants things as is, and deadened my heart, which is where desires and dreams unfold. The stories are the past and have no power over me any longer. From each story, there is a lesson well learned. It is the lessons that live on and shape who I am today. And I feel so blessed to have experienced what I experienced and learned what I learned for the purpose of helping others who are in this process.

I have a blueprint of plans for my future. I know roughly when I will retire from teaching. I know that I have saved enough money to be able to live comfortably in retirement. I know I will have lifelong medical coverage from my job. I am not sure about what I will "do" in retirement, but I know it will have to include helping others. In a few short weeks I will graduate from Yoga Teacher Training. I am the oldest one in the group of ten students – no surprise really, just makes me more badass I think. I am thinking about practicing yoga to hospice patients and others. I might live near a beach. I don't know. But thank you, forty years of therapy, for helping me get here.

I wrote this book to bring hope to others. These are my

experiences. They were not easy to live through. They were not easy to recover from. There are many people out there living isolated lives in hell, believing that they will never be free from fear or misery. Hear my voice.

Forgive yourself for not knowing more. Forgive yourself for any harmful things you think you have done to others. Forgive others for the awful things you think they have done to you. Perhaps they knew no better. Stop being a victim. Stop blaming others and take ownership of your own life. It is not disloyal to abandon your family. Your allegiance lies with yourself. Your duty is to love yourself and take care of yourself first. You are worthy.

There are times in our lives when we are so lost, so confused, and in such physical distress that we need therapy. Some people turn to God and receive what they need and move forward. Others, like me, have extraordinary faith in God, but are not able to sort through the muck or create recovery action plans without therapy.

"My gosh, she spent forty years in therapy. Didn't she know it wasn't working? Don't people do therapy for a shorter time and then live their lives happily?"

I actually hear these questions now that people know that I spent forty years in therapy. My answer is that for me, it took forty years to get to the point I am at now. Thank you God for giving me the strength to endure.

CHAPTER 2

The Tipping Point Workshop

I ARRIVED AT OMEGA Institute in Rhinebeck, New York in mid-July 2017 carrying two suitcases, one case of water, healthy snacks for the week, and a sack of journals and reading materials. I had already phoned twice for an agenda, each time being told that there is not a published plan. As a Type A personality with extra special control issues, I am amazed that I actually came without an hour-to-hour agenda and list of materials. My gut kept telling me that this is exactly where I was supposed to be. I was willing to surrender control (mostly) in the hopes of sending my fears packing for good and allowing myself to craft the life I hadn't yet even imagined.

I was assigned to a dormitory. For the next week, I basically lived in a closet and shared a bathroom with seven other women. My room had a bed, a nightstand, and a small hanging rack for a minimal amount of clothing. I couldn't comfortably turn around once inside. There was no TV. The only thing I was actually told was that each day would begin at about 6 a.m. and end at 10 p.m., so I wouldn't have recreational time for TV anyways.

There was one dining hall for all. I found it and came upon two women who looked as lost as I did. We realized that we are in the same class. These two women became instrumental to my healing during this conference. We were not lucky to find each other. We were destined to find each other.

One hundred two women met that first afternoon by the lake. I was thrilled to see Iyanla and her squad of warrior women. She looked just like she did on her own TV shows and on her book jackets, and her demeanor was no different than what I saw on her shows. We lined up, as instructed, in descending age order, which was no small feat for all these women. I was 59 years old, less than a month shy of being 60, and originally positioned myself in the 60's clan of women, but was told by Iyanla to basically get back to where I belonged in the 50s. But I didn't want to miss what was going to happen in the 60s group. What if there was some transformational material to be presented that I would miss? It made logical sense to me that since I was just a month shy of 60 I belonged in the 60's clan. Little did I know at the time that what I didn't learn in my 50s needed to be taught to me if I was to thrive in my 60's. Of course I did what she told me to do. I was all into whatever I needed to learn, and I trusted her with my well-being. This is saying a lot since I trusted no one ever, really.

Each of us had to pick a card from a very large bin, and this card was to represent our main issue or area to work on. My 50's clan sisters picked Alignment, Enthusiasm, Expectancy, Mercy, Honor, Determination, Trust, Forgiveness, Clarity, Choice, Presence, Purpose, Faith, Inner Cooperation, and Self-Awareness. I picked Truth. I suspected I was going to have to challenge the bullshit I told myself, among other things. There was some comfort in believing that you are less than. You don't have to challenge yourself very much. I was vaguely aware that this is how I felt and now drawing the "Truth" card brought that belief to the forefront. I had no idea what I was in for. The eldest sister in each clan became the clan leader and of course that was me. There was a ceremony to pick which one of Iyanla's squad of leaders would become our advisor. Ours was Iyanla herself. So our circle began with Iyanla, and then me Truth; next to me was Alignment, one of the women I ate lunch with. And next to Alignment was Inner Cooperation, the other women I ate lunch with. There were no coincidences.

I cannot tell you about the specifics of the workshop, because what happens in Vegas stays in Vegas, but I can give some flavor of what it was like and how I responded.

There was no fluff, ever. Every ritual, every exercise, every event was cosmically arranged for me personally. Or at least that is how it felt. Every other sister said the same thing. Can you get that? We were all where we needed to be and we were all willing to blindly travel on this journey. We understood somehow that this set of experiences was for our greater good– it was transformational.

One of my clan sisters was a commuter. She lived close by and would go home each night and research what we did. Each of the first few days, she would report back and assure us that we were getting sucked into a cult and getting brainwashed, but she kept coming back. She had other people on the outside doing reconnaissance work and after the umpteenth reference to God, we all relaxed and fell into the program. We knew that if we were praying to God and reciting Scripture we were in the right place.

I prayed and cried and prayed and cried the whole time. Had I known what the agenda was beforehand, I would have never attended, and Iyanla was smart enough to know that I am sure. I would have been too scared to even show up. Once it was over, I could not believe the things I did that were so out of my comfort zone.

Never once during this adventure did I experience a panic attack. The last big challenge did have me cursing like a sailor, yelling and screaming, and crying but I did not suffer a panic attack. I faced my fears directly. This last challenge was my turning point. This I can tell you more about.

We were directed to do something that was quite scary for me. We had to prepare ourselves before we did it, and it was during this time that I knew that I was at a crossroads. I felt emotions I had not felt since I was a little girl. I had to trust others to not judge me. I had to trust that I was good enough, even with flaws. I had to trust that I was worthy to live through this and that God would protect me.

As we traveled to the site of this experience, Iyanla would not take her arm off my shoulder. I am sure she thought I would bolt, and I may have. She was my guide, my anchor. When it was my group's time, I resisted. She talked me through the process and told me she would give me a choice to leave once everyone was in position, but until then I had to have my experience with dignity. I fought and fought and she just kept reassuring me she would give me a choice at the end. I listened to her voice and once we were all situated, she asked me if I wanted to leave.

I realized at that moment that I didn't know if I should stay or go, although I wanted to go. I was paralyzed. I felt that if I left, I was abandoning my clan and being disloyal. I was sure they would take away my leader status. You see, what I was experiencing at this moment was my past patterns with my family. Iyanla put me in a position that I was very uncomfortable with, and felt danger in, that mirrored my childhood.

Iyanla grabbed my arm and looked me square in the

eyes and said, "You have a choice, Truth. Make your choice, Truth. We all support you in whatever your choice is."

My life changed in that moment as I realized that as a child I had no choice or voice other than to do as told or else, and that I carried that belief into my adulthood. My adult decisions were made based on the expectations of others and the fear that if I did not do as they wished, I would be shunned from the group. Here, at this place and time, I realized that I had the power and right to make my own choice without repercussions from the group. They were telling me that I would still be their leader, their sister if I chose to leave. I wouldn't be ex-communicated.

I had to leave this hidden site to prove to myself that I could do what felt was right for me without fear, and that I would still be respected and accepted by the group. I spent about 10 minutes with the group at this place and then left. I waited on the outskirts for them to finish, and we all walked back together, with me at the head of the line as the leader. Iyanla was elsewhere. She didn't need to lead me home.

At the very end of the conference, I hugged Iyanla and thanked her. I asked her if she knew of a life coach I could hire. I told her my forty years of therapy were over and I was ready for intensive and quicker change. She pointed me toward a petite worker warrior. I had noticed her throughout the conference. She said very little, but carried a very big vibration. When I would cry, I felt her presence behind me.

She would squeeze my shoulder in reassurance. It felt like destiny. I feel blessed after each life coaching session with Reverend C., and empowered to enact change. And wow, have I made some changes. I am a different person than I was just two years ago before my Cape Cod writing trip.

I learned so much about many things during my time at Omega. One of my journal entries reads: "Today I found my voice. I won't remain loyal to them (my parents, my family). They don't want me for me. They want me for what they can get. I am no longer a soldier for them. I am no longer in danger. I am no longer powerless. I am an adult–safe." Another reads: "Do I use my stories as a crutch to stay stuck as a victim? I have to say it to heal. I need to heal the feelings that are attached to the stories. When these feelings come up, rat them out, Deb. I can neutralize them with new tools. Close my eyes and look inward to my heart."

I will not accept the stories as a lifelong condition. I am not helpless. The universe is so vast that it will give me back tenfold what I am willing to give up. My loyalty needs to be with me. I make up stories and convince myself they are true and live my life as if they are true. I use filters to see things. Maybe one of my filters is that I can trust no one and everyone is out to get me. I see people as threats and misinterpret their intentions as threatening, and then convince myself it is so, when it is not. What I mean by this is that although bad things happened to me, I used those bad things to tell myself that I deserved them, and that those types of things are the only things I should expect in life. I learned from forty years of therapy and this conference that I can acknowledge my bad experiences and then release their negative energy, applaud myself for surviving, and then thrive.

I refuse to make up shit that has nothing to do with anything. I am not unworthy or undeserving or fat or powerless or voiceless. I am using my voice today, in this season of my life, to expose some secrets. This is not a betrayal to my family, but an act of honor for myself. As I release this baggage, I make room for new wonderful things. Choice is powerful. Thank you Omega. Thank you Iyanla. Thank you God. And so it is.

CHAPTER 3

Friday Night Paychecks

NOTHING EVOKES A DEEPER sense of rage and fear in me than money. Nothing has had a more profound influence on my life than money. Friday Night Paycheck rituals have left scars. I suffered deep wounds that have taken a lifetime to heal.

My mom had an eighth grade education, and I don't ever remember her appreciating knowledge or academics. She never worked outside the home. She was anorexic, and then bulimic, and kept secrets. My dad perhaps had a GED diploma. He worked several jobs at the same time. He left for work around 6:30 a.m. each weekday and rarely came home before 9:00 p.m. each night. He worked Saturdays too, and Sundays most of the time. My dad was an overeater, rage-aholic, and kept secrets. I loved them both.

My dad got paid from his main job every other Friday. On paydays, he would come home from his second job early, somewhere around 7:30 p.m. The rituals would begin shortly thereafter. I recall being forced to be a participant beginning around the age of five.

Dad would come through the front door with a smile on his face and a pile of cash in his pocket. My mom would sit across from him at the kitchen table and I, placed between the two of them, would watch as he counted his money three times. He had to be sure that he had the right starting count. Each week he would ask my mom how much she needed for food shopping, and every Friday Paycheck Meeting she would tell him the same amount. He would count out the money for the food and place it in a stack on the table. He would ask about other spending categories and count out those totals. Spending categories were basic needs like food, shelter, electric, gas for his car, etc. He would then recount the piles two more times to make sure the count was correct. Sometimes he would make a mistake, and then he would put all the money back together into one pile and start over. Start overs were bad because they made him angry. If he had to do a double start over, he would almost weep in frustration. I would sit on the chair and pray to God that we wouldn't need a start over.

Once the piles for the regular bills were done, he would move on to "other expenses." Other expenses were not good, either. Things in the other expense category included birthday gifts, extra food money for holidays, clothes.

I clearly remember this one time when I was about seven that he asked my mother if I needed Easter clothes, and she said yes. He counted out the money for the Easter outfit, but then she added that I needed underwear. Underwear didn't fit into the Easter outfit category and he became very angry. I cried and told him that I didn't need new underwear.

Sometime later my mother and I were walking to the store and my underwear fell down to my ankles because the elastic was too broken to hold onto my waist. My mom had me kick them into the bushes. It was a windy day and I worried the whole walk that my dress might blow upwards and I would be exposed. My mother was in her own world and was only really aware of her own needs. She could not care about mine. I didn't think anyone else that was in my family would have cared if my dress blew up either.

I learned at an early age that my needs did not matter. I learned that I was not worthy or entitled to even have needs, and so I let them go, like my broken underwear.

Friends were not allowed growing up. Friends might find out secrets, like what happened during Friday Night Paycheck rituals. But there was this one time in eighth grade when I somehow managed to convince my mother that I could take a school bus to Joan's house, and that her mom could drive me home. I promised to stay only an hour. Joan lived in a real house, not a small apartment like the ones we lived in and had to move from each year. My parents never told me why we had to move frequently, and there really wasn't much notice any of the times, but I suspected that it was my dad's screaming and yelling that did it. I could be wrong.

I was mesmerized by Joan's house. It was huge. I never lived in larger than four rooms, and she had many more than that. I went into her bathroom and secretly looked behind the curtain. We never had a shower, only a tub. I was able to trace a fresh smell to a bar near the tub. I didn't know what it was until I asked Joan. It was a bar of Safeguard soap. We didn't use soap in my house, just water. This visit changed much for me. I realized that I didn't live like other children, and that maybe there was hope for something different. Once I knew that there was a new normal, I had hope that I could get it one day.

Friday Night Paycheck rituals took about two hours to complete. After the money was counted out, my mom and I would sit at the table while my father wrote down where every cent was going. If he made a math error on the paper, he would crumple the paper and start again. I held my breath each time the paper was tossed. When he was satisfied that his papers were correct, he would fold them into his wallet until the next paycheck. To the best of my memory, there was never a happy Friday Night Paycheck Ritual.

My dad kept the money he earned from his side jobs in his wallet, so that it always looked like he had hundreds of dollars in his pocket. My dad found great self-esteem and value in the money, and would take out his wallet when visiting his brothers and sisters, and show them how much money he carried, as if that would make him equal to or better than them. He would use this side job money for his food addiction.

Lack of money meant being less than, unequal to, and those feelings brought shame. My father could never have enough money to set himself free.

My mother and I would go food shopping on Saturdays. We would walk to the grocery store and take a cab home. My mother never got her driver's license, although she talked about getting it all the time–for years. I was not fond of this chore because we could only buy certain items. I learned to not ask for or suggest anything. I wondered why we bought dog food when we didn't have a dog–two cans a week. I knew I couldn't ask a question like that out loud or I would be hit, but I did one day discover what the dog food was for.

Several years later, when I was in my late twenties and living on my own, I got a bank statement in the mail on a Saturday from a bank I did not do business with. I opened it and discovered I had several thousand dollars in an account, and the bank was advising me to transfer the money into a higher interest account. I was shocked. I naively phoned my mother to tell her of my good fortune and she told me it wasn't my money. As it turns out, she used my social security number to open an account when I was a child to funnel part of the food money, along with "other expense money" for her own use, while my father worked all these jobs and she fed him dog food twice a week. On Monday the same bank called me and told that they regretted that I had withdrawn my funds. I did not know if my mother had herself as a co-signer on this account when she set it up and if she withdrew the money as herself after I called her, or if she pretended to be me. A daughter keeps her mother's secrets. I did not tell.

I have worked as hard as my dad for most of my life. Today, I say with conviction that money does not define me, or my worth. However, that was not true until very recently. In many ways, growing up poor gave me the perspective and belief that a lack of money equaled a lack of power. Lack of money increased my wants—wanting more food, wanting real clothes, a bar of soap, love. Determination and hard work drove me to be a straight-A student. I sensed at an early age that achievement was my ticket out of neediness. And so I achieved, and achieved to the point where I had a corner office with a fish tank, working as a middle-level financial manager in a good company. I worked full-time and went to college full-time.

I married a man I should not have. I purchased a large house with four bedrooms and literally constructed a white picket fence around it. And then, amidst the stress, busyness, and lack of center, I realized that all my money had not liberated me, had not made me equal, had not given me power. Instead the money became the walls of a prison that I created for myself. When would I have enough money? When could I stop being so tired, so disconnected, and so unhappy?

I stopped. I prayed. I reflected. In the middle of my divorce, I got sick from all the cruelty, punishment, and disrespect I showed my body. This forced me to reflect some more and reevaluate the money belief system that my life was built on—the life that I was once so sure would be made perfect with more money.

Over my lifetime, I developed very strict money rituals. I budgeted my money to the penny. I stockpiled food—real food, brand name food, Safeguard soap, and new and fancy underwear just in case I lost all my money and needed them. I ate hot dogs for weeks to save for the down payment on the house that I let go of during the divorce. I created twice-a-week money rituals where I checked my balances for accuracy and made sure my spending was limited. I became obsessed with making sure that I had enough money saved so that I would never be dependent on anyone ever in my life. My children did not know about my rituals. I gave them everything I could including beautiful birthday parties, sweet sixteen's, traveling softball memberships, cheerleading camps, countless dance lessons and recitals and costumes, trips to Italy, etc. They always had new clothes, especially loads of underwear.

I know now that I am resourceful, and that no one can steal my assets. I am self-sufficient and independent. I can buy not only what I need, but also what I desire. I appreciate listening to my heart–the heart that was hardened for decades. While I still check my accounts once a week, I know I don't have to. I have planned for a bright financial retirement because I learned how to live below my means while still providing self-care. It has taken me a long time to be grateful for Friday Night Paycheck Rituals, but I am now.

Money is not a measure of wealth or worth.

CHAPTER 4

Food Freaks

NEXT TO MONEY, NOTHING has conflicted my life more than food. My relationship with food has been complicated and confusing. I know that for some people, they eat food when they are hungry. It is nothing more than fuel for the gas tank. Other people really enjoy eating, not necessarily because they are hungry, but because they like tasting and experiencing new things. These people can turn the eating off. But for others, the tank is never filled because food serves as a very powerful tool to fill them up with what they are lacking in. My mom was anorexic/bulimic and my dad was a binge eater. They each had tormented relationships with food that shaped my own dysfunction with all things edible.

From a very early age, maybe four, I had the belief that I was fat because my mother told me I was. My mom would say, "What a pretty face you have." I hated that statement. It translates to: "If only you weren't so fat, you would be acceptable. If only you weren't so fat, you would be lovable. You are not good enough. It is such a shame." The few pictures I have of myself at that age prove that I wasn't fat. But I was not skinny enough for my mother's satisfaction. I could never be thin enough.

I didn't realize my mother was anorexic, and bulimic, until I was in my 50s and showed someone a picture of my mom from years earlier. They said "oh my gosh, was she always anorexic?" I took the photo to my therapist who asked me why I never told her that my mom was anorexic. It was that obvious to anyone, except to a little girl like me who grew up believing that thinness was a measurement of worth. I was shocked at myself for never noticing that she was too thin. I thought she was skinny, which was good, as opposed to normal or thick, which was me, and no good.

I can say now that she had an eating disorder stemming from before I was born. Many times she told me and others, whenever the opportunity arose to talk about weight, that she was 76 pounds when she became pregnant with me and that the pregnancy caused her to go all the way up to 130 pounds. She belittled that weight, as if 130 pounds was the size of a beached whale. She spoke of herself with disgust. But the conversations would always end with her boasting that she lost that weight quickly and never, ever allowed herself to go above 100 pounds again. My mom was about 5'5, and 100 pounds was way too thin.

Her thighs never touched. In fact, there was always a large gap between them. Her cheekbones were hollowed out and her eyes sunken inward with black circles underneath. She always had this odor that I can't accurately describe. She drank coffee like water. It was her breakfast every day. I don't remember her eating lunch or dinner until later, maybe when I was about eight or nine. She ate Entenmann's crumb cakes or cheese buns for dinner and would then go into the bathroom. I remember the sounds from the bathroom now.

There were cooking rituals. My mom would cook my father's dinner in the early morning, right after he left for work, and put it in the fridge. She would have me eat part of that for dinner at about 4:00 p.m. after she reheated the food. She would then leave the rest on the stove until my dad came home at night. She never ate what we ate.

A pretty clear memory for me happened when I was about 10 and noticed that dog food containers were in the garbage one morning. My mom was cooking her often made "hash." I don't know what allowed me to make the connection on that day, but I did, and never ate the "hash" again. My mother never asked why I didn't eat it, and never offered to make anything else either. I never even dreamed of telling my father. A child must keep her mother's secrets at all costs.

My dad, on the other hand, ate enormous quantities of food at particular times. He only drank coffee at home before he went to work, but I found out later in my life that he would stop at a deli in the town he worked in and get breakfast sandwiches every day. He would eat whatever lunch my mother gave him plus 12-inch deli wedges. Every night he would come home and sit at the kitchen table with his newspaper and eat his dinner. Sometimes he would yell that the food tasted like dirt, etc., but most times he would read and eat. By then it was around 9:30 p.m., and he would move into the living room, sit on the floor in front of the TV, and eat whatever else he brought home, and after that, whatever else he could find in the kitchen. This would go on for a few hours until he went to bed.

There was an unwritten rule that I could not talk to my father during his feeding times. I was aware by his vibration that he did not want to be disturbed. He would come in the door, go upstairs to wash his face and hands, and then come down to the same chair at the table with his newspaper. About an hour before he was due home, I would begin feeling unsettled and nervous. I knew by the way he shut the door whether or not he would be in a raging mood.

If it was a rage day, I would first try to divert his attention by smiling or trying to talk to him. This did nothing but frustrate him. I don't think my father was aware of the hell I lived in, because he was locked in a pattern of depression that didn't allow him to see beyond his own feelings most of the time. When he started to yell and scream, I would run into a closet and zone myself out. I know now it was a defense mechanism, inbred in my DNA to survive. On days when he wouldn't rage, he wanted to just be left alone with his food. The gorging was sometimes hard to watch, and it was hard to know when and if he was really done because it lasted so long. It was a tense world to live in as a kid.

It was also a very confusing world to live in. When I was with my mother, I ate alone. Eating was bad. I always felt judged when we would be somewhere and someone offered me good food, real food, and I said yes. I learned to sneak the food when she wasn't looking and quickly eat it. If she saw me eat it, she would stare. Later, she would ask me why I ate whatever it was. When I started to throw up each morning before school, it was not a big deal. She actually gave me the paper bag to throw up in, as I walked myself to school and off I went. To her throwing up was no big deal, but to a young child it was terrifying.

I learned how to eat quickly to hide what I ate, and always felt guilty about eating in general. However, when I was with my father alone, he would buy me food when he bought food. Sometimes, on a Sunday morning he would drive us to the bakery and buy cheese buns and crumb buns. He would let me eat however many I wanted before we got home to my mother. Maybe once a year, we would go a nice restaurant in town and eat out–my dad, my mom, and me. We would get dressed up and pretend to be happy and go to the restaurant. My dad would let me drink a "Shirley Temple," which was really just ginger ale with a real cherry in it. I would always order the turkey dinner because it came with a roll and mashed potatoes with gravy. I don't recall at all what they ate because I was so focused on my own food, my own portions. I would eat enough to make my dad happy, but not enough to make my mother be embarrassed of me or risk getting hit when I got home.

My dad showed his love for me by buying me food and allowing me to eat excessively so that he could eat without guilt in public, and my mom was always disappointed in my failure to not eat it. Everyone in my father's family ate big. When we would visit my grandparents, the first thing my grandpa would ask is, "Dolly, do you want some eggs?" I had a nickname and the offer of freshly made eggs. My mom never made eggs because she said the pot would be too hard to clean. Of course I would say yes, and he would offer me toast or bacon too. It was a favorite place for me to go for many reasons. I thought they saw me as a real person who might want some eggs. They played cards with me just because they wanted to. I think they actually loved me. I know my grandpa did. But I could not share my secrets with them. There was a clear vibration that there was a difference between my father and the rest of their children. My dad always seemed to be an outcast. It was not until I was much, much older that I asked why my father had a different last name than my aunts and uncles. I was never given an answer, ever. After my dad died I did my own research and found out that he actually had their last name until he was drafted and found out that no such person existed. At age eighteen he learned his mother's birth name was his legal last name and not the name he was raised with.

Holidays were a nightmare—all of them. They were filled with contradiction and heartache. Religious education in second grade taught me that Christmas time is supposed to be filled with love and hope at the birth of our savior. Each year I would fill with anticipation that this Christmas would be different—an event free of violence and terror. And each year, Jesus did not save us from the torment. It would always start with the food. My dad would make lists of foods to be purchased and prepared. My mom would buy the generic brands and cook them, I think, as best she could. But she was never able to please my dad or his appetite. Something was invariably not hot enough, not tasty enough, not big enough, and there would be total disappointment from my dad. His frustration led to yelling and screaming and ranting and raving, which led my mom to the same. No one was ever invited to dine with us, not on holidays or ever, and we were not ever invited anywhere to eat.

I wasn't allowed to leave the table until my dad was exhausted from raging, because if I left sooner, he would blame my mom for ruining my Christmas. He played the role of victim very well. This would only heighten his emotions. I learned to just sit very still at the table with my head down until he stopped screaming and began gorging the food. Once he was settled at the table and began reading the paper, I would go into my bedroom and hide. After he finished eating, he would go right to sleep and then wake up a few hours later and yell again and eat again. This cycle continued over and over.

Thanksgiving and Easter were the same, always.

The first time I joined Weight Watchers (WW), I was 14 years old. Over the course of my lifetime, I have joined this program a total of four times. I joined the cheerleading squad in high school, without my parents knowing, and became captain in my senior year. Looking back, I was not heavy in high school, but I thought I was a fat slob. I have never been comfortable in my own skin—not when I weighed 110 pounds and looked like a bag of bones, or when I was 170 pounds and looked soft in the middle.

I remember being a senior in high school and on the WW plan. I was a perfect member until this one day when I ate an extra apple in error. When I realized it in the evening, I felt like a total failure. I laid down on the floor and hooked my feet under my bed and did sit-ups until my stomach cramped so hard, it brought me close to tears. I needed to get rid of that apple. I knew my emotions were out of control and that I was acting irrationally, but it didn't matter. It was as if at that moment I was possessed.

My weight has fluctuated over my lifetime. However, for

the past 12 years, I have only had a 10-pound weight range change. But this stability has not come without sacrifice. I believed that I could conquer my food addictions and consistently follow a food plan. I also joined Overeaters Anonymous and worked very hard in that program as well. Every Friday, I plan my meals for the next week and food shop. I spend several hours on Saturdays preparing my food for the week, packaging everything, including snacks. For 10 of the 12 years, my compulsion for food preparation, tracking every bite, drinking 80+ ounces of water a day, and exercising nearly every day has served me well in that my weight was stable, ranging from 143-146.

But during the last year and a half, I have struggled with my weight. My goal weight was 150 and when I began approaching it, I persuaded my doctor to write a note to WW indicating that 155 should be my goal so that it could be raised according to their rules. I have gone as high as 157 and boycotted the meetings so that my weight could not be recorded. I took pride in never, ever, ever being over my goal and now wear the weight with shame—again.

On Weight Watchers foods have points. I know the point value of every food I eat, might eat, and once ate. I know which exercises burn the most calories. I know about the weight loss value of water and sleep and stress. I am an expert at riding the fence—overeating but over-exercising to compensate. I can spot the difference between 3/4 and 2/3 of a cup a mile away. I know a lot. But my knowledge is based on the premise that I can control it all to a result I desire. The more I try and control, the more powerless I learn that I am.

In my heart, I know that the weight gain has very little to do with what I eat, or how many miles I walk in a day. I have followed the plan perfectly and still gained weight. I have eaten next to nothing and still gained weight. My weight is tied to my emotional baggage.

I am courageously working very hard on releasing my emotional baggage. The weight does not serve me. I realize that I no longer need a protective barrier on my body. I am out of danger. I have put down my sword. The war is over. Food is not my enemy or my ally.

I began making changes a few months ago. I am departing from my lifelong beliefs about food. I am opting for peace. For the rest of my life, I will cook healthy food dishes as I have for a long, long time. Healthy is good. Healthy shows self-love. I am an incredible cook. You can also bet that I will continue to drink my water because it is good for me, as is healthy exercise and portion sizes. What is different now is that when I feel like gorging on high fat or high calorie foods I ask myself why, and if I can't arrive at a plausible reason I don't eat them. I also weigh myself just once a week or every two weeks instead of daily. I no longer write down everything that goes into my mouth. I trust that I know how to eat healthy and that I love myself enough now to do it. I am working on being free from the compulsions and obsessions that have haunted my eating habits. I no longer need to eat a meal and immediately start thinking about the next one. There is a new ease at mealtimes.

I am a work in progress. I am sure that I have driven my daughters crazy with my food freak mentalities. I apologize to them for placing so much value on weight. I realize now that being a lovable person, a worthy person, has nothing to do with weight. For each secret I release I will lose weight. For every caring act I do for myself, I will lose weight.

I forgive my parents for training me as well as they did in regard to food. I don't think that either recognized their food behaviors, or the effect they had on each other and me. Food was a tool they used to punish themselves, rather than face whatever they needed to face. Alcoholics can remove themselves from alcohol. Drug addicts can remove themselves from drugs. But food addicts cannot remove themselves from food.

It took a lot of work, but today I enjoy holidays. I don't anticipate them with dread. I continued to believe that each holiday might be different up until the day my dad died, but they were all the same. When I married I created spectacular holiday affairs but they weren't authentic. Today, I appreciate the significance of each holiday and value the time with my daughters. I think that only by the grace of God have I turned out to be a kind and loving person despite my food freak issues.

CHAPTER 5

The Pin Cushion

MY GRANDMOTHER'S NAME WAS biblical, which is truly ironic because she was the furthest thing from the Blessed Mother than one could imagine. She had four children: Susan was the oldest daughter, Katherine the next oldest daughter, my mother, and a son, the baby of the family named John. My grandfather died in his early thirties during an asthma attack. My grandmother was left to raise four children on her own, without a job or an education.

No one in my mother's family graduated from high school because my grandmother needed them to work and bring money into the household. The allegiance was with the family. I'm told my Aunt Susan never worked, but I don't know why. My Aunt Katherine worked two jobs all of her life and I will tell more about her in another chapter. My mom stopped working when she married my dad and moved out of her family apartment. My Uncle John worked his whole life. During the brief period of time he was married, he still supported his mother. My mother's family did not like my dad, but then they did not like anyone outside of the "family".

My dad had bouts of depression and rage. Sometimes the rages would last for weeks. I always wondered how he was able to hold two jobs and not get fired, but he had the longest longevity of any employee at both jobs when he died. It wasn't until many decades later that I came to understand how abusers could appear normal, if not stellar, to the outside world—outside of the family.

The summer I turned nine was an especially tense time in my household. My mother planned a birthday party for me in August. She bought a tablecloth, paper plates, and cups that matched, even napkins. She set up a picnic table in the backyard of the apartment we were renting at the time. I wore a paper crown. No one showed up. I am not even sure if she actually invited anyone. My mother then wrote in the newspaper that she had hosted a ninth birthday party for her daughter at her residence. She cut it out and put it in a frame that she gave to me. I had to keep it on my bureau. This became a repeating ritual. It has taken me decades to willfully celebrate my birthday as an adult. I have thought about this on and off over the years and can't come up with a reason why she did this. It was cruel after the first time.

My dad struggled more than normal this particular

summer, and the depths of harm deepened during his episodes. My mother and I walked each day to my grandmother's apartment where we would have to spend the day. Good daughters did as told. I absolutely hated going there for many reasons. My mother would need to retell my father's behaviors to her mother and her sisters, who in turn would tell her what to do back to him for revenge. One day my grandmother called me into her bedroom. I don't believe I was ever allowed anywhere except in the kitchen or on a plasticized couch in a living room. She presented me with a pin cushion filled with pins. She directed me to stick my father hard with a pin whenever he yelled at my mother.

Although by age nine I had developed an exterior of steel, and rarely showed true emotion, and always followed orders, I resisted this order. My grandmother became enraged and demanded that I do it or I would rot in hell. I took the pin cushion and put it in a pocket. I felt terror walking home with my mother. I prayed that my father would not be home, or if he were home, that he would be nice. This was just a few days after my "party". We cut through the woods and in the clearing, I could see his big old Pontiac in the driveway. My heart raced and I felt sick.

The entrance to our apartment was on the ground floor and we had to climb a large set of stairs to get into the apartment entrance door. My mother made me open the first door and I saw my father sitting on the top step, leaning against a wall. He was drunk. My father almost never drank. I was paralyzed and my mother shoved me up the stairs. He had lost the house key somewhere and was waiting for my mother to open the door. She did and he fell asleep in his bed immediately.

In my closet, I thanked God for my good fortune; my closet was my sanctuary. I would use the closet in the many apartments we lived in as my prayer space from an early age. When there was domestic violence, I would hide in there and pretend that I was in a confessional at church and that there was a priest with me. I would confess all my sins and promise not to commit them again if God would stop what was happening. I felt safe in there.

I can't remember what happened to the pin cushion after that day. I am reasonably sure I never stuck him, or at least I would like to think I never did. I never spoke to my grandmother again, except to answer a question when she asked.

Children are dependent upon the adults they are forced to trust. I was helpless and a victim of manipulation. I had no choices. I had to comply or be beaten. Comply or not be fed. Comply or be imprisoned. But what I gained through these experiences was inner strength. I am a warrior that can withstand pain that others cannot. I am a rock in a crisis. I am strong. I am compassionate because I know what it feels like to live like a less than. Adults—pay attention to what you make your children do or let them see.

People can't give you what they don't have. My mom wasn't able to parent me better than she did, nor was my dad. I get that. But what was harder to accept was that other family members were complicit in guarding the secrets. An army of enablers offers no protection to a wounded child.

CHAPTER 6

Furniture Rituals

HAVE YOU EVER THOUGHT about the purpose of furniture? I have thought about it repeatedly for years because of my Aunt Katherine. Aunt Katherine, as I was told, was once in love with a soldier who died in a war. She remained unmarried, and never dated again, not even once. Aunt Katherine always worked two jobs for as long as I can remember. Her main job was with a very large utility company.

Her job function was to connect people via the telephone— an old fashioned, now defunct job. It seemed as though Aunt Katherine had a considerable amount of extra time during her workday to do "dirty business." She unethically listened to family members' phone calls. More often than not, you would be able to hear the slightest "click" if you were on the phone with someone, which indicated that Aunt Katherine was listening in.

A braver pre-teen might have looked at these situations

as opportunities to really make Aunt Katherine's hair stand on end. I used to fantasize about what I could actually say while on the phone that would make her jaw drop, or worse. But I rarely used the phone, and when I did, it was only for a specific purpose that was short. I remember my mother at times setting her up. I watched with fascination at how my mother would weave a web of deceit to trap Aunt Katherine and call her out on her eavesdropping, which today might be a felony offense.

The result of Aunt Katherine's listening skills ended in arguments, screaming matches, and always forgiveness, so that the whole process could start again. It was sort of like an intricate dance. My Uncle John never said a word to anyone–only whispered to my grandmother and never talked on the phone. Some of us learned to "not be heard."

Aunt Katherine also worked at night at a local psychiatric facility, which was so ironic. Irony pervaded my mother's family. She worked the overnight shift as an orderly. When I was a child, she and Uncle John supported my grandmother financially. Her money also went to a peculiar habit: furniture.

Aunt Katherine, Grandma, and Uncle John lived in three different apartments over time, that I remember. Each apartment was larger than the one before, even though it was only the three of them together. Each apartment was more stuffed with furniture than the one before. There was not more than a few inches of wall space around the perimeters of each room that did not have a piece of furniture, or an ornament of some kind. The living rooms sometimes had two or three expensive couches in them, covered in plastic.

Such enormity of furniture and baubles required intensive cleaning. These items seemed to me to be replacements for the man never married, and the children never born. They were very cherished things, to be protected and admired. My Aunt Katherine spent most of her limited free time performing inspections and furniture rituals at home. Let me explain how this went.

She would change into her duster and slippers and bring her supply bucket into the living room, which was always the starting point. The bucket had cleaning supplies and two flashlights, along with batteries. Even in broad daylight, she would turn on the flashlight and get down on her hands and knees to inspect every inch of every piece of furniture. Scratch polish was in the bucket, and if she found a ding or scratch, she would fill it with scratch polish as she cried. She would spend hours on that room, and rant and rave and cry about its imperfections. There always had to be a villain who damaged her things. The dining room was next, and then the bathroom and kitchen. I never knew what happened in the bedrooms because those doors were always locked to prevent family intruders.

I would have to move from the kitchen to the bathroom as she cleaned. Watching these ritualistic behaviors as a kid was confusing. I never understood why the furniture was more important than the people. I never understood why I had to watch it as a witness. I never understood as a kid why she wept and yelled as she did it. I absolutely hated her. God forgive me. She was the most visibly sick person in the family. I must confess that there were times when I would intentionally sneak into the living room and kick a chair. I never got caught. The few times that company was invited into the house, always cousins from "the city", she would stare them down as they sat on her furniture covered in plastic. When they left, she would do an even more intensive cleaning/purging.

Grieve your losses. Every lifetime has losses. When we discount them, ignore them, and pretend they don't matter, they can morph into things like Furniture Rituals.

Place value on people and not things. Things may not hurt you, but they can't love you. I have learned that there really are only two emotions–love and fear. When we live in fear and place our trust in things, we miss out on love. I've learned that when you live to love and place your love in people, you experience less fear and compulsion.

Stop and look at your behaviors and ask if they are harming innocent people. I was an unwilling participant in these rituals, but my aunt's compulsion to do them was much stronger than any feelings for me. My mother and grandmother's comfort in this insanity prevented them from any awareness that it was wrong. My being part of this ritual was just expected.

One of the biggest reasons I disliked Aunt Katherine was that she had this neediness about her that suckered people in. She was sneaky and manipulative. While all my aunts and my uncle and grandmother were self-absorbed and selfish, Aunt Katherine out of all of them was the coldest. I don't think she ever touched me – hugged or kissed or ever sat with me or even talked to me other than to give a command. I think she actually hated me and every other person who entered her living room.

It took me a long time but I forgave my Aunt Katherine and understand that she did the best that she could with what she was taught and believed to be true. Her behaviors were not corrected or challenged, and she was never given the emotional and mental support she needed to be well. All these years later I am very aware when I buy a new piece of furniture. My home is not crowded, in fact I would say I am somewhat of a minimalist. Thank you furniture rituals for teaching me that things are not a measure of worth and love.

CHAPTER 7

The Slitting of the Wrists

MY MOTHER'S YOUNGER BROTHER John was the baby of the family. He was over six feet tall and couldn't have weighed more than 150 pounds soaking wet. I don't think I heard him speak more than 20 words in all the years that I knew him. He would take my grandmother, mother and I out for Sunday afternoon rides each week for years, and rarely said a word. If someone asked him a question he would answer with a nod.

There were certain family rules that had to be followed in regard to allegiance and loyalty. As my grandmother's child, you were never allowed to leave her nest. Even if you married, you stayed. One rule was that if you slept somewhere else, you had to phone her once in the morning and once at night. You had to visit her each day. As her only son and her baby, Uncle John had to eat breakfast and dinner with her. He was allowed to eat lunch without her, but only if forced to by work. My uncle worked for the same company his whole life.

It was expected that he would never marry. At least that is what the family expected. My grandmother required that he remain single so that he could live with her and support her as Aunt Katherine had. It came as quite the shock when he told my grandmother he was dating a woman, born from another country–a woman with a college degree. I remember when he brought her to meet my grandmother. My grandmother pretended to faint and the meeting ended. My grandmother argued for days, but then a few months later he married the college woman and they rented an apartment right above the apartment my grandmother and Aunt Katherine lived in. He would come to my grandmother's for breakfast and dinner and take the lunch she prepared him to his job. He continued to take my grandmother on her weekly Sunday afternoon drives. I was about 10 years old when they married.

I think I was the only one happy about the addition of this woman to the family. She looked normal. I was pretty sure she was normal, at least at the start. My mother kept saying that she was a drunk because the country she was from "breeds alcoholics". My mother also called her a whore because she went to college. I didn't believe any of that.

Aunt Joyce worked each weekday and allowed me to visit her often. She taught me so many things. She could play the piano. She was the greatest chef. I could not understand as a child why my uncle would eat anywhere except in his own home, with meals prepared by his own wife and not his mother. I didn't understand much at all about why she would marry him in the first place. She had fish tanks and furniture I could actually sit on. She didn't care if I spilled something. She was a crafter. She smiled. I loved her.

Over time, I began to see sadness in her eyes. I began to understand that it was only a matter of time before "they" would steal her soul and destroy her. It took a about a year but I watched the light go out in her eyes. My uncle spent more and more time with his mother. They all undermined her, including my mother, at every opportunity. She was less than and not a part of.

It was Father's Day. I don't remember the year exactly, but I know that I was around 11. My cousin Manny would have been about nine. Manny was my best friend, my only friend, an adopted son of Aunt Susan. We shared secrets together. We never talked about them, but we lived them. Manny went to the emergency room a few times as a kid from "falls." I was told that I would be beaten if I told anyone "the truth," so I always sat quietly at the hospital waiting to hear if he was dead or alive.

This Father's Day we went over to my Aunt Susan's house. My grandmother and Aunt Katherine lived right across the street. As I said before you never leave even if you get married. Aunt Susan could not have children. I often thought it was because God didn't want her raising any children. She adopted two children; one a beautiful girl, and later my cousin Manny who she told everyone was Italian, but was really Puerto Rican – a fact she could never accept and a fact that he paid dearly for.

My father was wearing a brand new white shirt and he hadn't gotten upset all day. Manny's dad was also wearing a white shirt. Aunt Joyce came in the front door crying. I had never seen her cry before. She was very upset. She was upset about the way my uncle was tied to my grandmother. My grandmother, who was also there, started screaming at her that she was not going to take her son away. My uncle just stood there paralyzed. There was screaming back and forth as the other aunts and my mother joined in the gang attack.

Aunt Joyce ran into the bathroom and locked the door. My uncle asked her to come out and she refused. Then Manny's dad and my father banged on the door telling her to open it. There was no answer back. They broke down the bathroom door and found that Aunt Joyce had slit her wrists. Manny and I hid under the coffee table in the living room and played cards as they carried her out with blood spurting all over. The white shirts were ruined. Manny's mother had no choice but to call the police. We continued to play cards as the ambulance took her away. No one ever asked if we were okay. No one ever explained what happened. No one ever cared about us.

My father was very upset about his ruined shirt and Aunt Susan was mortified that her neighbors saw what happened. It ruined the facade she had created. Aunt Joyce was sent to an institution to recover. I overheard my family telling the authorities that she stole drugs from her job and was a drug addict. I didn't believe any of this to be true. My Uncle John continued his silence but when Aunt Joyce recovered and went home, she became pregnant. She had a beautiful baby. Unfortunately the birth of this baby only escalated the family's need to remove Aunt Joyce.

One of the most difficult times of my life was the months spent listening to my mother's family plotting to run away to another state to steal this child away so that Aunt Joyce would not see her. You see, I think my family believed that children were possessions to be owned. Aunt Joyce was outside of the family and a real threat because she was educated enough to know her rights. If she decided to leave my uncle, she would take the child with her and my family would not allow that. There was never discussion about Aunt Joyce's feelings or those of my cousin.

I pleaded with my mother to stop them, but she wouldn't. In fact, that led to my exclusion from all conversations. I was a danger. And then one day my grandmother, Aunt Katherine, Uncle John, Aunt Susan and the child were gone. Aunt Susan returned a few weeks later but the rest never did.

Aunt Joyce begged my mother to tell her where they went and she wouldn't.

Aunt Joyce tried to commit suicide one more time. I visited her during her last confinement, as I was old enough to drive and had purchased an old car for myself while still in high school.

I found her in the center hall of this large building playing the piano. She played beautifully. She could barely speak. I think she knew who I was but there was no conversation. That was the last time I saw her. Shortly after she was released her life ended. Her dad came to America to take her remains home, and he had coffee with my mother at our kitchen table. My mother sung Aunt Joyce's praises and insisted that she had no idea where her family went. I sat across from him speechless. After all the horrible things that I lived through with my mother, nothing prepared me for what I witnessed that day. She was perfectly calm and convincing in her story. She was a master at her craft. And I considered myself her dutiful accomplice. I felt trapped like a rat in a corner. If I told him she was lying, I didn't know what would happen. I would be disloyal to my awful family. But if I didn't tell him, I would have to live with more shame and guilt. I didn't tell him that she knew where they went.

My family never knew that my Aunt Joyce gave me several of her personal items – the things that mattered to me and represented our relationship. She gave me her cookbooks and secret recipes and directions on how to make certain handmade items. I cherish them still today.

With the help of modern technology I was able to find out where my mother's family ended up, including my mother. One day my mother just vanished from the house I helped buy for my dad. My dad's sister called to ask me where my mom went, and that's how I knew she was gone. After my family left with my cousin I never heard from them again. My mother kept in contact with all of them. I married and carried on with my life including my mother in it, until it became harmful to my children.

My mother's behavior grew more and more bizarre over the years before she left. She sued me for harassment and claimed that I went to her home and threatened her. Good thing for me I was working at my job and could prove my whereabouts when the police summoned me. And then she was gone. She sold the house and vanished.

I now know that she moved to this other state and into a senior facility until she accidently set her kitchen on fire. She was then moved to a more restricted environment. She suffered from mental illness and then dementia. I have a high school friend that actually worked in that facility and assured me that she lived well there.

I will never forget the day the wrists were slit, nor the day my Aunt Joyce's dad came to claim her body and try to find his grandchild. Manny and I were traumatized and left playing cards under a living room table. At that time, I was a trapped, helpless, and powerless girl. I felt like I had no choice, in the same way I had no voice. It never occurred to me that I could be disloyal to the family. It was an impossibility then. It took me a long, long time to believe that I was worthy of a life on my own terms. Sometimes I stop breathing when I accept that I am a survivor. God gave me this testimony so that I could be compassionate to others in need. And I am forever grateful.

CHAPTER 8

The Cheesecake

IF THERE IS ONE thing that I am very good at, and always have been good at, it is cooking and baking. Aunt Joyce taught me the "How To's" of both, and I still use the recipes from the bequeathed secret cookbooks. I am grateful to her for being willing to teach me what no one else was able to.

I was a quick learner. Over time I learned how to modify and create my own recipes, some of which are still incredible 50 years later, if I do say so myself. Cooking and baking gave me meaning and worth to the people in my family; well, some of them.

The motivations for learning how to cook and bake are a bit complex. I didn't think this consciously at the time, but now I suspect I worked very hard at being very good at this so that I could soothe my father and his binge eating. My dad's binge eating brought him relief from suffering as no other crutch could. He could come in the door raging, but quickly calm down if he was fed something he craved. My mother repeatedly fell short with this task because of her own food rituals, and this consistently set off my dad.

One day as a freshman in high school, I had an especially heavy feeling of impending doom and decided to try and preempt it by making my father the best tasting cheesecake he had ever had. Cheesecake was never in our house due to the cost, but I bought the ingredients and the baking pan myself from the money I earned from a part-time job at a nursing home, and meticulously prepared it with a lot of hope that it would be a sacrificial lamb to my dad and prevent something bad from happening.

The cheesecake was almost perfect. It was a good five inches high and smelled heavenly. The imperfection was that the top dipped ever so slightly in the middle. It was almost an invisible dip. My father came home agitated. I felt anxious again. He ate his dinner and then I brought the cheesecake to him at the table. With naivety and hope I presented it to him, explaining how I had made it for him.

He looked at it, and put his head down and then shook it, as in no. For a moment I thought he was going to cry, but with the saddest eyes he told me that it wasn't good enough. What I heard him say was that the dip in the center made it ugly. I read his emotion as pure frustration that even a cheesecake couldn't be good in his life. He threw the cake against the wall.

My mother shot me an "I told you so" look, not for my benefit, but to try and align me with her. She didn't defend me or scold him. It felt like she was basking in the glory of perhaps gaining an accomplice. I thought I saw a smile. This was one of the few times I cried. I can't remember crying at all past age seven or eight because I had developed an armor of steel. But I cried at this moment, on this day.

All hope was gone in those moments. I realized that I would never be good enough for either one of my parents, but it would take decades for me to stop trying. I was alone, truly alone as a 14 year old. A door shut–tightly. I disassociated with the two of them. I said hello and goodbye but did not share or try to share any information about me or school because neither one had an interest. I don't think they even noticed. I stopped baking for my dad. What I didn't realize then was that God had given me a tremendous blessing. Had my dad appreciated the cheesecake, eaten it with calm satisfaction, I would have associated it with my being able to redirect his behavior. The truth is that I couldn't have ever prevented an outburst or attack.

The cheesecake incident was a blessing for another reason as well. It gave me the impetus–the proof–that I needed to plan for my future. College was a possibility because I was smart. I thought that maybe I could earn enough scholarships to pay my way, but attached to the dream of going to college came the reality that my mother would disown me. She believed that only whores went to college away from home.

A few months thereafter, my mom announced she was pregnant. She was 42 and less than 100 pounds. I was shocked by this news because anyone witnessing my parents together would have thought that they were destined to kill each other and certainly were not ever having sex with each other. But much bigger than that was my reality that I could never escape or be saved because I would choose to be a protector for my sibling. I felt guilty for a long time that my disconnection from my mother led her to get pregnant and create another victim.

Although most of my mother's family had hidden themselves away in another state, and therefore the risk of my sibling being abused as I was lessened, my parents' individual bad behaviors had actually escalated. I felt a sense of responsibility. No one helped me, and I could not leave my sibling defenseless. I made the decision to forego my future until the point that my sister could take care of herself. I never spoke to her about my childhood. I was always in the shadows to step in and defend her, which I did many times. People thought that I was her mother when we were together. We never experienced a sisterly relationship. I do not know how to fulfill a sisterly role.

It's taxing and tiring to live a life on defense. I am a master at anticipation. I can plan six steps ahead of a current move and foresee every possibility in a situation, and be prepared to respond effectively. This makes me a very good manager and leader. It has served me very well over the years. But it also made me a good ninja warrior. There are very few personal situations that require ninja reactions anymore, but for me, being in a constant state of heightened awareness was my normal. It took decades to become mindful.

I know now that I am good enough. It took me 50+ years to believe this, but I am. The cheesecake was more than good enough. Some people stay entrenched in their own misery, blaming everyone else for their circumstances. Some people should never parent. I don't have to rise to other people's expectations of me. Someone's love for me should not be dependent upon my usefulness to them. I am never responsible for anyone else's behavior. I am grateful for being taught these lessons. I am a great observer and listener. I could never have honed these skills if I lived a different childhood.

Over the years I have baked many a cheesecake. I am grateful I never made a "perfect" one. I smile every time I see a crack or a dip because it reminds me that God loves me with my flaws. I have never tried to disguise the imperfections with berries, and I hope I never will.

CHAPTER 9

10/28/88

OCTOBER 28, 1988—IT WAS a beautiful morning. In fact, it was probably one of the best days of the year weather-wise.

My childhood was spent in a state of perpetual fear, yet I deeply loved my father. In my heart, I always considered him to be a victim, although he was not. I suppose all my childhood alone time with my mother highlighted how cunning and manipulative she was. I was aware, somehow intuitively at first, that her behaviors were not okay. As I watched my father fall prey, so to speak, and was unable to use my voice to warn him or protect him, I lived in shame. I cried guilty tears and spent years trying to make it up to him. My need to break away and save my own life was not as important as trying to help my dad. Although he hurt me in many ways, I would always let him off the hook. It is very difficult to live with secrets, especially when you are a powerless child.

I believe my dad never felt good enough for his family. When he discovered he did not share his family name he was told that he was only illegitimate on paper, but that the dad that raised him was really his biological dad. He was told they simply did not get married. He wondered why they never changed his name legally. There were many questions that he did not pursue answers for. I sought those answers in his memory and have them now. They would not have soothed his soul.

There was a few times during my childhood that my dad and I got away from my mom and had some alone time. His anger was always directed at my mother and not me directly. The cheesecake incident was the only time he directed anger directly towards me, but even that I later regarded as anger at his imperfect life and not at me directly. In actuality it was his rages at my mother, his family, his life that did the most damage to me. I was collateral damage. I didn't feel scared being alone with him. However, I always felt anxious because I knew that when we got back home, and my mother got me alone, she would beat me for going with him.

My father always spoke about his being less valued and less important than other people when he spoke of not owning a home. I co-signed for a small house he could call his own when I was in my early twenties. He made a garden in the backyard. Over the years, he taught me how to fish, how to garden, and how to appreciate nature. One thing we shared each Sunday night was time watching *Wild Kingdom* on Channel 2. To this day I watch as many nature shows I can. I still stand in awe of the ocean and the mountains and God's animal kingdom.

I made sure to speak to my dad often after I moved out of the house, even if it was only for a brief hello. I moved out when I was seventeen, and then moved back in when I co-signed for his house. I moved out for good when I was about twenty-three. The offering of the house was like my penance – for the pin cushion incident, for wishing him gone many times so that there could be quiet, and so that he could find peace. He always said he would die young, and I always thought that he would, due to his size and eating and working habits. I didn't know when it would happen, but each year I thought it would be that year.

The few weeks prior to 10/28/88, I did not speak to my father. He was on my mind often those two weeks. I couldn't quite put my finger on why. I was very busy with work and he continued to work two jobs. He never missed work at either job—ever. Neither did I.

I awoke agitated that morning. The sun was shining brightly and there was warmth in the air. I was out of sorts, which was unusual for me, a morning person. I lived about 10 minutes from my parents and about 20 minutes from my job. When I started to drive to work, my agitation grew. I had substantial chest pains. It felt like an elephant was sitting on my chest. There was an unusual traffic jam on the highway and I had to pull off to the side. Right behind me was a co-worker who pulled behind me to check on me. I told her that my dad had just died and asked if she could tell my boss I would be delayed. I knew my father was dead. I can't explain how I knew, but I knew. I drove to my parent's house and saw my dad's baby-blue Cadillac in the driveway. He should have been at work hours before. I unlocked the door and his dog Barney was sound asleep in his bed at the bottom of the stairs. I called out "Dad?" There was no answer. I knew he was dead upstairs. My mother was not at home. I drove to work.

My boss was shocked to see me. I told her what happened and asked to use her phone. Cell phones were uncommon in 1987, so I needed a landline to try and find my mother. I was determined to find my mother to make her go home and deal with my father. In my heart, I knew it had to be her. I spent all my life parenting my parents, and this was a pivotal moment when my mother had to be a wife. It was a life-long pattern for both parents to tell me their "sides of the story". I can remember these talks, as far back as maybe when I was four years old. My mother would tell me how other people were harming her and what I needed to do to be a loyal daughter. My father would tell me how my mother ruined his life and how he was so depressed. I took on the role of parent, trying to make life as easy as possible for them and making excuses for their behaviors. I would buy my dad things he never would for himself – like new underwear, new clothes. I would insist on doctor's visits. I would take my mother out to different places. I would buy her things. After I moved out she would call me several times a day and I would listen each time.

I found my mother at her friend Mina's house. I asked her where my dad was. "That lazy s.o.b. didn't go to work. He's sleeping in bed." "He's dead in the bed," I said.

"No he isn't, I vacuumed around him and he's sleeping in the bed." I repeated that I was sure he was dead. She said she would go home and wake him up and call me back.

She called back to say, "I can't get him up, but he is not dead." I clearly remember being in a controlled rage as I spoke to her. Her continued denial that he was not dead was absolutely on target with who she was. The sky could be blue and my mother would insist that it was brown, and that the people who saw it as blue should be tarred and feathered. Her disconnect with reality served her well over the years as it got her off the hook and other people did for her what she did not want to do herself. But this time – it would not work.

"If you can't get him up, he is dead", I said.

She asked what I wanted her to do. I told her to call the police.

I have no idea what was driving my behavior or my words, as I can't recall having any active thinking at all. I hung up and my boss told me to go, and I did. I drove back to the house and saw the EMTs leaning on their ambulance, idling on the side of the road. I parked and asked how my father was. They told me he had been dead for some time. I asked them how long that meant and they told me he had been dead for at least eight hours, which meant that he died in the bed next to my mother.

When I went inside, my mother was on the phone with her sister, my Aunt Susan, who she assured me for years she hadn't spoken to, asking her to come get her to take her to the bank. A neighbor came over and I asked her to get my sister from the high school. I would not leave my father alone in the house again. The EMTs explained that they could not remove the body, and that I had to wait for a coroner to come and pronounce him dead. Then the body could be removed. The coroner was playing golf and I had to wait.

My mother went to the bank to withdraw all the money from all joint accounts, as is customary in my family, and I waited. Hours later, I went to the neighbor's, as suggested by the people moving the body, as they removed my dad. My father was a very large man, and they dropped him as they tried to get him down the stairs. I remember the broken railing when I came back into the house.

I made all the calls to his employer, friends, and family. His sisters and brother came to the neighbor's house. They didn't cry at all. My mother was crying and I was very angry with her. I suspected the worst. She treated him like a dog and now she was crying over her "loss." I remember one of my father's sisters saying that she had to leave to give herself a manicure. These were the people that I thought were "normal". These were the people who I aspired to love me and save me. Yet the announcement of the importance of a manicure jarred me into realizing that who they were and who I pretended they were did not align.

My husband cleaned the bedroom, disposed of the sheets, etc. We slept in the living room that night and the next day I made the arrangements for the funeral. My mother took possession of all his things, except I fought her for the wallet. I took it after she took the money out; she only wanted the money, not the wallet. His wallet was filled with his lists and pictures of my sister and me. Once a year I take it out, and after nearly 30 years, it still smells like him. I also took all of his many keys. I mounted them in a shadow box last year. His keys were sort of like his trophies. Each key represented the level of trust that his employers had for him.

She fought me on the autopsy, and as his wife she had control over the decision. I am unsure how he died. His death certificate indicated "suspected massive heart attack". My dad also left a legal-sized pad with lists with my name on it in a drawer. It explained how often to clean the gutters, mow the lawn, plant seeds, etc. I followed his instructions on this pad for a long time. I became the keeper of the house, which included paying for repairs, etc.

He was buried on Halloween. I put a sign on my parents' door asking the trick or treaters to not ring the bell, as there was a death in the family. I stayed over that night as well. My husband and I paid for renovations for the bedroom so that my mother could see it differently. I am amazed looking back that I took so much time and care to take care of her during this time. I can only explain this care I gave my mother as a continuation of the parental role I took on years before.

I was very concerned about my sister's welfare. I made sure that she acquired the money from the sale of my dad's car that I sold, as well as other monies. I gave up any rights to any money whatsoever. That is what a good soldier does.

There were many, many mourners. My father knew a lot of people through his jobs. He was a hard worker who did his best at his jobs always. I felt his loss deeply. I know that he loved me the very best that he could. I know that he did not intentionally set out to hurt me. He was a very depressed man. (The most educated person on my mother's side of the family was her second cousin Jenny. She was a licensed social worker and therapist and visited my house a few times over the years. She told me that my father was bi-polar and my mother's whole immediate family had mental health issues. She advised me to get away but I did not heed the warning.)

A few weeks after my dad's death, I had a "visitation"

from him through a dream. I was in a hospital waiting room and my father was being worked on behind these swinging doors. It was so quiet you could hear a pin drop. In the dream, I was consumed with fear and dread until my dad's spirit came through the doors and spoke to me. He looked so calm and peaceful and free. He told me that he was happy and safe. He told me not to grieve, but to celebrate his passing. He said it was a blessing. And then he was gone.

When I awoke, I promised myself that I would not work two jobs like my father and miss my future children's lives. I promised myself that I would not be consumed by money, or use money as a measure of worthiness. I promised myself that I would take time off work if I were sick. I promised myself that I would lead a happy life, one in which I followed my heart.

I broke each promise, except I was a big part of my children's lives. It is only now that I am able to fulfill these other promises to myself. It has taken me 30 years to understand that I do not have to follow my dad's legacy. I am not being disloyal by doing something different.

Both my parents had choices all along the road of life. The decision that they both made was to stay together. If my father was a victim, he chose the role, and the same goes for my mom. Back in the sixties and late-fifties, couples did not get divorced. I remember visiting one of my parents' few friends occasionally, and the wife frequently had a black eye.

No one ever said anything about it. There was a brief time that my parents were separated. I was really little, maybe three, and my mother and I ran out of the apartment in the middle of the night and to my grandmother's house. We were both hysterical because my dad was so out of control. We stayed there for about a week or so, but then my mother returned to my father.

Every October 28th, I pause and reflect on my dad. I don't think I will ever be able to reconcile how I knew that he died other than to say that we were deeply connected. I felt his pain on many levels. Although there are many bad memories, I believe that he could not help his behaviors. He was trapped with no foreseeable way out. I can honor him by living my best life and breaking the cycle. I am helping to save the planet and respect nature. I am doing my best in all things. I am honoring and loving myself, and others. I blame no one for my mistakes or failures. I forgive others and myself.

My father indirectly taught me how to be compassionate toward people who have emotional and mental disabilities. My father taught me how to work hard. My father taught me that everyone has a story that they believe to be true. My father taught me that things are not necessarily as they appear to be. My father taught me that everyone wants to be loved and accepted. My father taught me that I couldn't be perfect enough to make someone love me when they are incapable of loving. My father taught me that a child should never have to act as an adult or parent their parent. Almost all the lessons he taught me were done inside out. That's what I call them. He didn't directly teach me. I learned the lessons based on observing his destructive patterns and seeing the depths of his despair.

My father is loved, not because of what he did or did not do. He is loved because he is my father.

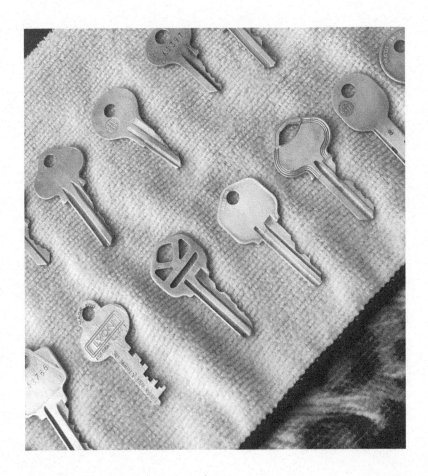

CHAPTER 10

My Resurrection

MY CHILDHOOD WAS CHALLENGING. My adulthood has been complicated. Many times I felt unqualified to live in a human world. I grew up missing the basic foundation of life skills that other children learn by having positive adult role models. The lessons that I was taught did not align with skills needed for me to be the best that I could be. My lessons learned taught me how to be a survivor, how to protect myself, and how to live in a sustained state of stress. These are not bad skills, but without counter balancing lessons about how to love and value yourself, how to receive and give love, how to follow your heart, etc., I have lived in a scary and unsafe world.

I have lived in a constant state of confusion and anxiety, although my tough exterior would never clue you into that. Truth and vulnerability have been two of several traits that I learned could be deadly, but now embrace them. Survival has been dependent upon my ability to play my cards well, through strategizing and planning. It has been a tiring way to live. I rarely, if ever, felt safe.

Over the years, and with forty years of therapy, intuitive and observation skills, innumerable self-help assignments and readings, and most importantly, conversations with God, I have been able to poke holes in my thinking and crack myself open. I have transformed myself more than a few times. I know what I know and then stay quiet and listen so I can find out what else I don't know. As I gain knowledge about the lessons lost, I get stronger. I learn and integrate.

After high school, I stayed in close proximity to my sister so that I could be available to her for safety. I attended college part-time and worked full-time. I took three classes at a time, graduated with an associate's degree and a 3.9 GPA and then a bachelor's degree in business administration, also with a 3.9 GPA. It took me 10 years, but I persevered. I valued education, and instinctively knew that no one, ever, could take away my degrees. I continued to go to school for several more years, earning more and more certifications. At one point in my adult life, I had a room filled with my framed accomplishments—awards and designations for this and that. It was my room of fame. I needed to display my awards so that I could remind myself daily that I was accepted and valued. Eventually I learned that these accolades did not measure my worth or worthiness. I took them all down and have no idea where any of them are now. They are meaningless to my state of being today.

I married a man for the wrong reasons. He loved me and accepted me as the agoraphobic woman that I was at the time. He stood by my side and helped me through many hard spots. Over the years, as I grew stronger and healthier, we grew apart. We had children, a house, a picket fence, and at the end, we still fought although not as my parents did. I remember a crossroads as being the day he never showed to pick me up from the hospital after my mini-stroke. I took a cab home. We were together for 28 years. I wish him well today and forgive him for things he did that I consider hurtful, and hope that he forgives me. We have been divorced for about 13 years.

I have had some wonderful corporate jobs, having worked for some of the nation's top companies in various capacities. I traveled for my jobs and enjoyed being a boss, being responsible for managing millions of dollars. I thrived in high-stress jobs that others may have found overwhelming. I was trained well.

When it became clear to me that I needed to divorce in order to teach my daughters that we are responsible for our own destiny, and we all have the right to be safe and live in a peaceful environment, I knew that I needed a more stable job. My girls meant the world to me. They did not ask to be born, like I did not ask to be born. I was determined to give them a stable life. I thought staying in my marriage so long fulfilled that, but it did not. I never really mattered to myself. I volunteered to sacrifice myself so that they could think that they were safe. Over time and new lessons learned, I realized that they needed me to be the positive role model, and I owed it to myself to be safe. There was a strong sense of being responsible for breaking the cycle. It was a huge responsibility, but I knew with God's help that I was the one that had to do it.

There were times I empathized with my mother. She may have felt trapped. She had no education, no means of support, an unsupportive family, and a set of old life tapes that limited her strength. In my family it was understood that there would never be discussion ever about growth or responsibility or accountability. There was never the thought of conflict resolution when there was a disagreement with outsiders. You simply cut them out of your life. They were always to blame. Good soldiers also did a lot of pretending. If things were bad you pretended they were not. If underwear fell off you simply kicked them under a bush and pretended you were still wearing them. If no one attended a party you pretended that they did. Do you get this?

When I told my mother I was divorcing, she was very mad. She asked me who was going to change her screens each year if my husband was out of the picture. Who would fix her house when there was need? Who would drive her around? She made it clear that she would align with my ex-husband because he was more useful to her. And she did, and he fulfilled that need. They continued this relationship for a few years, until the day she vanished.

I decided that teaching would be a good career for me. I suspected correctly that there was little difference between managing adults and managing children. I was a teacher to my subordinates and their coach/facilitator. Teaching had similarities. I knew that I needed a job that could support myself and my children and that required no travel. Teaching also provided great work hours.

On purpose I teach in a district with tough kids. My city has been named the gang capital of the state more than once. It makes total sense that I would choose to be here. The harder the kid, the more motivated I am to teach. I can't imagine any joy in teaching an honor's class. My intention lies in teaching the hardest kids that they are loved, capable, and worthy. I teach the kids that few want to teach. I consider teaching to be my calling because I do God's work in the classroom. I am a boot camp-type of teacher, in some ways similar to the way Iyanla managed me. I lay out the goals we must accomplish and demand nothing but their best work. They don't ever come to me with excuses after the first month of class. They learn that they are responsible for their successes or failures—no one else. They learn that my expectations are very high for them, but doable. They know

I would not ever ask them to do something they are not capable of doing. They know that I love them and have their backs. They know I get their world.

I have been called grandma more than once by accident, and each time, I take it as a compliment. Grandma in many of my student's world, is the leader of the clan. She is a hard-nosed, tough, God-fearing woman, who loves her grandchildren deeply. I appreciate that title.

When you teach, you are never quite sure of your impact on students because the results sometimes take years to manifest. Teaching is an isolating profession. I am all about effectiveness and progress on many levels, but once my door is closed, I can't compare my results to other teachers. And that is such a blessing for me. I stay in my own lane. State test results mean absolutely nothing to me. I teach kids who may never, ever pass a state exam. State tests are not disability friendly. They do not measure the worth of my students. Yet these results are worth 50% of my rating as a teacher each year. Again, this is such a blessing to me because it verifies that my worth as a special education teacher has nothing to do with these grades. The cheesecake was good enough–get it?

I have learned how to navigate the level of my sacrifice in teaching. This could be a dangerous profession for someone with my history, and there have been times when I have had to pull back and evaluate my motivations. Am I trying to save them? Am I trying to save the little girl in me? I have learned how to get very, very clear about my intentions. I used to also home teach kids thrown out of school as a second job, but don't anymore. I once had five part-time jobs in the district, in addition to my regular teaching job. I did that for a number of years, but as I learned more, I understood that that level of busyness and distraction is not good for Deborah.

Today I have one full-time teaching job and a few small part-time jobs that don't negatively impact my time. One of those jobs, not surprisingly, is a contract negotiator for the teachers union. I mean how could I not? Negotiators strategize and plan and use game face—c'mon!

I have learned lessons about balance. I am a spiritual, emotional, physical being, and today I value and respect each part of who I am. These lessons have been hard for me to learn, and God has given me several opportunities for growth in this area. For decades, the things that mattered most and motivated me were things that provided security and safety. I never wanted to be dependent on anyone for money. I never wanted to be trapped in relationships. This fear has driven the amount of education I have given myself, the size of my bank accounts, the size of my retirement funds, the amount of healthy eating and exercise that I do, and other similar items. Today I am confident that I have done all that I could to provide for myself. I won't be a burden to my children. I have given myself permission to relax in this area.

Relaxation is not something that comes naturally to me. It still sometimes feels wrong, but I have come to understand that things that don't produce a tangible result, like relaxation, are exactly what I need to nurture. This year, I approach each school day as an opportunity to do good. I have taken away any pressure to be the voice for the voiceless. Instead, I teach the kids how to develop their own voices.

My God is very important to me. About six years ago, I left my lifelong allegiance to the Catholic faith and joined a church that values relationships with Jesus and the Word of God. I am a Born Again Christian. My Bible studies and church-goings have taught me many of the missing lessons I searched for my whole life. There is a universal law that states that God comes first, then me, then family and friends, and finally work. I have learned to find peace in my life by honoring God first, and then myself. Work has always come first in my life because I thought it provided the safety and security I needed to not feel vulnerable or at risk. As I became aware of my imbalances I was able to release many of my part-time jobs. Now I know that God always has my back and loves me unconditionally. It's about faith and trust.

I was always last on my list. I was "loved" as long as I was useful. When I refused to conform to other's expectations, I became disposable. I was thrown out like garbage repeatedly. It was not until I learned to value and love myself that others began to value me, not for what I could give them, but for who I am. I have nothing to prove to anyone anymore. I am good enough as I am. I don't need permission to live my life freely. I don't need approval to feel validated.

In some ways, I never lived for myself until very recently. When my youngest child left my home, I lost my purpose. My anxiety and panic attacks, which I thought I had conquered, re-emerged with full force. After my divorce, my focus was on my girls. I lived through their lives. If they were successful, I felt successful. If they had challenges, I blamed myself. I understand now that their successes and failures are their own. They were raised by a village of people, not just me. What they do or don't do is not reflective of my parenting skills. I did the best I could, without a manual, or role model.

Today, I have a life. I have some really authentic and fulfilling friendships. My forty years of therapy have ended and have served me well. Thank you, Patty. We do touch base with one another about once every few months. We are more like friends than anything else at this point. I plan to work with my life coach Reverend C. a bit longer. I feel excited about the future and what I can do with it. I know that I desire to live near the water—could be a lake or the ocean. There is energy in that water that inspires me—always has. I know that the townhouse I have lived in the last thirteen years since my divorce is a fine place to live. I have spent a lot of time visiting prospective places but nothing has touched my heart yet. The urgency to find a place is gone. I have thrown it out into the universe to find. And I am totally confident that it will show up one day.

I followed my cracked open heart this past fall and enrolled in a yoga teacher certification course–200 hours. Graduation is May 6, 2018, one week from today. This was a huge undertaking. After I listened to my heart, I paused to listen to my mind. This certification process took a lot of time, commitment, and determination. I doubted my physical, mental, and emotional ability to do it. I am sixty years old. But in the end, I pushed myself off the cliff and completed it. This is probably the first time I did something that defied my reasoning. My thinking plan is to teach yoga as another career. Maybe I will have my own little studio, or maybe I'll go to the waterfront to teach. But wherever it is that I teach, I will bring love and acceptance.

I am ready to let someone special into my life. My armor is off and I have put down my sword. Today I can imagine that it might be quite nice to have someone care for me, love me as I am, support me, have fun with me. My girls are fine. They are exactly who they are supposed to be. They are each on their own journeys as they should be. I don't need to run interference. I trust that they will do what they feel is best for them (and not me). And this is as it should be.

Up until the last year or so I basically have been afraid to let God lead my life <u>fully</u>. God has always been next to me, and I have always been willing to let him into my life, and there have been times when I have fully surrendered to Him. But there have also been times when I have pulled back and took back control when I was fearful. I know now that I have never been the one in control, as much I would like to think so. I have been consumed by filling up all my spaces with things and doings, and have not created room to receive whatever life may offer me. I have lived a limited life.

I have freed up space by releasing some fears and old beliefs. And I have opened up space by writing this book and releasing some secrets. I would love to say that I am a "free spirit" because it sounds so delicious, but I am not quite there yet. Maybe I not meant to be a free spirit. I am a happy work-in-progress. I am aware of when I am feeling an emotion from an old story because my body tells me. When I am tense or having an ocular migraine I know my body is telling me to pause, breathe and figure out how I am dishonoring myself. Then I make the correction and move forward.

Although born without a thoughtful first name, my last name is repeatedly called class after class, day after day, year after year by my hundreds, if not thousands of students – hey Ms. Bouley. Even my colleagues call me "Bouley". Rarely do I hear reference given to my first name. Call me Deborah. Call me Truth. Call me Salina. I am all. The greatest name that I can call myself is "child of God", and in Truth, Merciful, I am.